# Tips On Parenting Child With ADHD :

## keys to raise a child with adhd

*By*

**Prince Bills**

# TABLE OF CONTENT

# Introduction

## How to help your child with ADHD

Life with a kid or adolescent with attention deficit hyperactivity disorder (ADHD or ADD) may be challenging, even overwhelming. But as a parent, you can assist your kid to overcome everyday problems, redirect their energy into constructive fields, and bring more tranquility to your family. And the sooner and more consistently you treat your child's difficulties, the higher chance they have for success in life.

Children with ADHD often show deficiencies in executive function: the capacity to think and plan, organize, regulate impulses, and finish activities. That means you need to take over as the executive, offering extra supervision as your kid eventually gains executive skills of their own.

Although the symptoms of ADHD may be nothing short of aggravating, it's crucial to remember that the kid who is ignoring, offending, or humiliating you is not doing it purposefully. Kids with ADHD want to sit quietly; they want to keep their rooms neat and orderly; they want to do whatever their parents ask them to do—but they don't know how to make these things happen.

If you bear in mind that having ADHD is equally as irritating for your kid, it will be a lot easier to react in good, supportive ways. With patience, compassion, and lots of assistance, you can manage children's ADHD while maintaining a stable, happy family.

**ADHD and your family**

Before you can effectively raise a kid with ADHD, it's necessary to understand the impact of your child's symptoms on the family as a whole. Children with ADHD display a host of behaviors that may disrupt family life. They frequently don't "hear" parental instructions, thus they don't heed them. They're chaotic and often distracted, leaving other family members waiting. Or they start tasks and forget to complete them—let alone clean up after them. Children with impulsivity difficulties sometimes interrupt discussions, demand attention at unsuitable times, and speak before they think, saying tactless or humiliating things. It's frequently tough to get children to bed and to sleep. Hyperactive youngsters may rip about the home or even put themselves at bodily risk.

Because of these behaviors, siblings of children with ADHD encounter a variety of obstacles. Their needs typically receive less attention than those of youngsters with ADHD. They may be scolded more forcefully when they misstep, and their triumphs may be less appreciated or taken for granted. They may be engaged as helper parents—and blamed if the sibling with ADHD misbehaves under their watch. As a consequence, siblings may find their affection for a brother or sister with ADHD mingled with envy and anger.

The rigors of supervising a kid with ADHD may be physically and psychologically draining. Your kid's failure to "listen" may lead to irritation and that frustration to anger—followed by guilt over being upset at your child. Your child's conduct might make you concerned and upset. If there's a core difference between your personality and that of your kid with ADHD, their conduct might be very tough to tolerate.

To tackle the difficulties of parenting a kid with ADHD, you need to be able to master a balance of compassion and consistency. Living in a household that gives both love and structure is the greatest thing for a kid or adolescent who is learning to manage ADHD.

# 1

## Stay healthy and positive yourself

As a parent, you set the setting for your child's mental and physical health. You have control over many of the elements that might favorably affect the symptoms of your child's illness.

Maintain an optimistic attitude:
Your finest assets for helping your kid handle the difficulties of ADHD are your positive attitude and common sense. When you are calm and concentrated, you are more likely to be able to connect with your kid, enabling him or her to be peaceful and focused as well.

Keep things in perspective:

Remember that your child's conduct is due to a condition. Most of the time it is not deliberate. Hold on to your sense of humor. What's humiliating now may be an amusing family anecdote ten years from now.

Don't sweat the minor things and be prepared to make some concessions

One duty left undone isn't a huge concern when your youngster has finished two others plus the day's schoolwork. If you are a perfectionist, you will not only be continually unsatisfied but also establish unattainable expectations for your kid with ADHD.

Believe in your child:

Think about or make a written list of everything positive, valuable, and unique about your child. Trust that your child can learn, change, mature, and succeed. Reaffirm this trust daily as you brush your teeth or make your coffee.

Self-care:
As your child's role model and most important source of strength, it is vital that you live a healthy life. If you are overtired or have simply run out of patience, you risk losing sight of the structure and support you have so carefully set up for your child with ADHD.

Seek support:
One of the most important things to remember in rearing a child with ADHD is that you don't have to do it alone. Talk to your child's doctors, therapists, and

teachers. Join an organized support group for parents of children with ADHD. These groups offer a forum for giving and receiving advice and provide a safe place to vent feelings and share experiences.

Take breaks:

Friends and family can be wonderful about offering to babysit, but you may feel guilty about leaving your child or leaving the volunteer with a child with ADHD. Next time, accept their offer and discuss honestly how best to handle your child.

Take care of yourself:

Eat right, exercise, and find ways to reduce stress, whether it means taking a nightly bath or practicing morning meditation. If you do get sick, acknowledge it and get help.

# 2

## Establish structure and stick to it

Children with ADHD are more likely to succeed in completing tasks when the tasks occur in predictable patterns and predictable places. Your job is to create and sustain structure in your home so that your child knows what to expect and what they are expected to do.

Tips for helping your child with ADHD stay focused and organized:

Follow a routine

It is important to set a time and a place for everything to help the child with ADHD understand and meet expectations. Establish simple and predictable rituals for meals, homework, play, and bed. Have your child lay out clothes for the next morning before going to bed, and make sure whatever he or she needs to take to school is in a special place, ready to grab.

Use clocks and timers

Consider placing clocks throughout the house, with a big one in your child's bedroom. Allow enough time for what your child needs to do, such as homework or getting ready in the morning. Use a timer for homework or transitional times, such as between finishing up play and getting ready for bed.

Simplify your child's schedule

It is good to avoid idle time, but a child with ADHD may become more distracted and "wound up" if there are many after-school activities. You may need to make adjustments to the child's after-school commitments based on the individual child's abilities and the demands of particular activities.

Create a quiet place

Make sure your child has a quiet, private space of their own. A porch or a bedroom works well, as long as it's not the same place where the child goes for a time-out.

Do your best to be neat and organized

Set up your home in an organized way. Make sure your child knows that everything has its place. Lead by example with neatness and organization as much as possible.

## 3

## Encourage movement and sleep

Children with ADHD often have the energy to burn. Organized sports and other physical activities can help them get their energy out in healthy ways and focus their attention on specific movements and skills. The benefits of physical activity are endless: it improves concentration, decreases depression and anxiety, and promotes brain growth. Most importantly for children with attention deficits, however, is the fact that exercise leads to better sleep, which in turn can also reduce the symptoms of ADHD.

Find a sport that your child will enjoy and that suits their strengths. For example, sports such as softball that involve a lot of "downtime" are not the best fit for children with attention problems. Individual or team sports like basketball and hockey that require constant motion are better options. Children with ADHD may also benefit from training in martial arts (such as tae kwon do) or yoga, which enhance mental control as they work out the body.

## ADHD and sleep

Insufficient sleep can make anyone less attentive, but it can be highly detrimental for children with ADHD. Kids with ADHD need at least as much sleep as their unaffected peers but tend not to get what they need. Their attention problems can lead to overstimulation and trouble falling asleep. A consistent, early bedtime is the most helpful strategy to combat this problem, but it may not completely solve it. Help your child get better rest by trying out one or more of the following strategies:

**Decrease television time** and increase your child's activities and exercise levels during the day.

**Eliminate caffeine** from your child's diet.

**Create a buffer time to lower the activity level for an hour or so before bedtime.** Find quieter activities such as coloring, reading, or playing quietly.

**Spend ten minutes cuddling with your child.** This will build a sense of love and security as well as provide a time to calm down.

**Use lavender or other aromas in your child's room.** The scent may help to calm your child.

**Use relaxation tapes as background noise** for your child when falling asleep. There are many varieties available including nature sounds and calming music. Children with ADHD often find "white noise" to be calming. You can create white noise by putting a radio on static or running an electric fan.

## 4

## Set clear expectations and rules

Children with ADHD need consistent rules that they can understand and follow. Make the rules of behavior for the family simple and clear. Write down the rules and hang them up in a place where your child can easily read them.

Children with ADHD respond particularly well to organized systems of rewards and consequences. It's important to explain what will happen when the rules are obeyed and when they are broken. Finally, stick to your system: follow through every time with a reward or a consequence.

As you establish these consistent structures, keep in mind that children with ADHD often receive criticism. Be on the lookout for good behavior—and praise it. Praise is especially important for children who have ADHD because they typically get so little of it. These children receive correction, remediation, and complaints about their behavior—but little positive reinforcement.

A smile, positive comment, or other rewards from you can improve the attention, concentration, and impulse control of your child with ADHD. Do your best to focus on giving positive praise for appropriate behavior and task completion, while giving as few negative responses as possible to inappropriate behavior or poor task performance. Reward your child for small achievements that you might take for granted in another child.

## 5

## Help your child eat right

Diet is not a direct cause of attention deficit disorder, but food can and does affect your child's mental state, which in turn seems to affect behavior. Monitoring and modifying what, when, and how much your child eats can help decrease the symptoms of ADHD.

*All* children benefit from fresh foods, regular meal times, and staying away from junk food. These tenets are especially true for children with ADHD, whose impulsiveness and distractedness can lead to missed meals, disordered eating, and overeating.

Children with ADHD are notorious for not eating regularly. Without parental guidance, these children might not eat for hours and then binge on whatever is around. The result of this pattern can be devastating to the child's physical and emotional health.

Prevent unhealthy eating habits by scheduling regular nutritious meals or snacks for your child no more than three hours apart. Physically, a child with ADHD needs a regular intake of healthy food; mentally, meal times are a necessary break and a scheduled rhythm to the day.

- Get rid of the junk foods in your home.
- Put fatty and sugary foods off-limits when eating out.
- Turn off television shows riddled with junk-food ads.

- Give your child a daily vitamin-and-mineral supplement.

# 6

## Teach your child how to make friends

Children with ADHD often have difficulty with simple social interactions. They may struggle with reading social cues, talk too much, interrupt frequently, or come off as aggressive or "too intense." Their relative emotional immaturity can make them stand out among children their age, and make them targets for unfriendly teasing.

Don't forget, though, that many kids with ADHD are exceptionally intelligent and creative and will eventually figure out for themselves how to get along with others and spot people who aren't appropriate as friends. Moreover, personality traits that might exasperate parents and teachers may come across to peers as funny and charming.

*Helping a child with ADHD improve social skills It's hard for children with ADHD to learn social skills and social rules. You can help your child with ADHD become a better listener, learn to read people's faces and body language and interact more smoothly in groups.*

- Speak gently but honestly with your child about their challenges and how to make changes.
- Role-play various social scenarios with your child. Trade roles often and try to make it fun.
- Be careful to select playmates for your child with similar language and physical skills.

- Invite only one or two friends at a time at first. Watch them closely while they play and have a zero-tolerance policy for hitting, pushing, and yelling.
- Make time and space for your child to play, and reward good play behaviors often.

www.ingramcontent.com/pod-product-compliance
Lightning Source LLC
LaVergne TN
LVHW052115160826
845678LV00015B/3563

* 9 7 9 8 3 5 3 3 8 8 2 8 9 *